MONEY MATTERS

18 STRAIGHTFORWARD RULES FOR FINANCIAL GROWTH AND STABILITY

Felix Makanjuola Jr

By accessing these pages you shall be deemed to accept and agree to be bound by the terms of this notice.

A number of the ideas described in this book relate to different types of investment regulated by the UK Financial Conduct Authority (FCA). Felix Makanjuola Jr is not regulated by the FCA and nothing in this book should be regarded as an offer or solicitation to conduct investment business or buy or sell any investment, nor does it constitute any form of personal recommendation

© Copyright 2016 Felix Makanjuola Jr
www.felixmakjr.com

All rights reserved. No part of this publication may be reproduced, distributed, or transmitted in any form or by any means, including photocopying, recording, or other electronic or mechanical methods, without the prior written permission of the publisher, except in the case of brief quotations embodied in critical reviews and certain other noncommercial uses permitted by copyright law. For permission requests, write to the publisher, addressed "Attention: Permissions Coordinator," at the address below.

The Base Media Publishers
19 Dan Danino Way
Swansea, SA6 6PJ
www.thebasemedia.com

ISBN: 978-1-908243-05-8

Printed and bound in the United Kingdom

"... It's not how much money you make, but how much money you keep, how hard it works for you, and how many generations you keep it for."

– Robert Kiyosaki

CONTENTS

Preface   9

Rule #1
Every money decision has a cost of its own   13

Rule #2
Never put your wants above your needs   17

Rule #3
Talk about money and be honest   21

Rule #4
Stop trying to impress other people   29

Rule #5
Spend less than you earn   35

Rule #6
Plan ahead before You spend   43

Rule #7
Open an emergency fund   49

Rule #8
Eliminate (and avoid) high interest debt   59

Rule #9
Make sure you invest   67

Rule #10
STOP WASTING TIME   77

Rule #11
TAKE CARE OF YOUR THINGS   89

Rule #12
DO IT YOURSELF   95

Rule #13
FIND AND WORK TOWARD YOUR TRUE PASSIONS   101

Rule #14
BUILD REAL FRIENDSHIPS AND RELATIONSHIPS   109

Rule #15
IMPROVE YOURSELF EVERY CHANCE YOU GET   115

Rule #16
MAKE GIVING A LIFESTYLE   121

Rule #17
HAVE A SAVINGS PLAN   127

Rule #18
TRACK YOUR PROGRESS   133

GLOSSARY   139

Preface

Have you ever felt that life did not always give you what you wanted or even what you seem to deserve? Bad things seem to happen to good people and good things seem to happen to bad people. Have you ever wondered what the whole point of life is? Sometimes when you seem to do the right things, that's when the negative happens and the reward of your labour doesn't seem to match your input.

You see as a lad growing up, my father enjoyed luxurious years of working in an executive capacity in one of the world's leading oil and gas firms - Mobil Oil. At some point, my dad felt a change of vocation into pastoral work. I can't remember exactly how dad painted the picture to the family but I got a sense that this was an exciting new journey that will come with new positions and promotions, a life of more luxuries and unlimited resources to tap from. I was barely a teenager at the time and little did I know many of my assumptions were incorrect and in most cases a farce.

Fast forward a few years, all the comforts I had become accustomed to were all gone, we were living on very little, of which we still had to share the little we had with many who were less privileged. In many instances I had to share my father also, with the many people who wanted him to help them in one way or another. So, you see , the experiences I went through had painted my reality and it wasn't a good picture.

I had tasted wealth and poverty in a very short space of time and I came to the conclusion that I preferred the former. As early as 16 years of age, I began looking at ways to turn around my fortunes and get out of the poverty predicament.

I started seeking advice and help from everyone and anyone around me that would offer it. I looked to those I perceived were financially successful. I was introduced to some guys who were driving fast cars and wore flashy clothes. I wanted to be like them. I wanted to know how they were doing it being that we were in the same age bracket. When I moved a little close to them, I realised it was a life of crime and deception. Also, I figured I was too good looking for prison and I wouldn't do very well locked up. I didn't want that, surely there must be a better way out.

I started studying entrepreneurs and celebrities alike. I wanted to know, what attitudes they had that seem to make them a magnet to money. This wasn't too hard I approached a handful of people, dug into their personal lives, read books in order to understand how this money thing worked.

At age 18, I remember approaching a young man by the name of Christopher (Chris) who had recently joined a local church in my area; he was in his early twenties. Chris was quite successful financially. He had a good job with a reputable company, Hewlett Packard (HP), he had a company car, company phone etc. He was already on the property ladder and with just 6 years between us, I was quite impressed!

Amongst many things, Chris helped me understand a few things about money. I still remember how he coached me on things to look out for when looking to buy a property. For example, he taught me that a property is only worth as much as the buyer is willing to pay for it. With this knowledge, I was able to detach myself from materialism and unnecessary sentiments. So, by the age of 21 I had bought my first property. I went ahead to acquire even more properties, even in the heart of London Docklands; and even bought a piece of land in Africa; all these before I was 25.

Along the way, some mistakes were made which cost me hundreds of thousands of pounds, but most importantly lessons were learnt and I want to share my experiences with you. I decided to write this book to encourage and help you; to help you to reflect on the changes that you want or need to make. This is not about a New Year's resolution. In order to make this work, you have to see it as a lifestyle change. It's not about making a quick buck because if you follow the simple rules laid out in this book, you will make a quick buck. However, what is harder than making money is maintaining it.

In this book, I explore practical tips on how to make money and how to hold on to it. You don't have to be a financial analyst to understand the principles being discussed in this book; it is straightforward and can be adapted to your particular financial goals. Whether you want to get out of debt, maintain your wealth or increase your worth. In this book you will realise 18 money rules to keep in your tool box.

Whether you want to get out of debt, want financial freedom, want to grow your wealth or you are preparing for retirement and beyond, this book is for you. Inside, I have laid out practical tips which you can follow as a step by step guide to help you meet your financial goals

Are you ready to begin the journey? Sit back, grab hot drink, and get ready for me to help you transform your life for the better.

Rule #1

Every Money Decision Has A Cost Of Its Own

When it comes down to personal finance, one economic principal rules the roost - opportunity cost. With more household incomes stretched to the limits in the wake of the global economic slowdown, this principal is quickly becoming a budgeting essential. However, the rule doesn't just affect what we spend our money on - it also dictates much of our personal finance lives. From our careers and our individual housing situations to how we invest and where to go to school, understanding the opportunity costs concerning these decisions is key for a sound financial footing.

"Opportunity cost," very simply, means what we give up to get something else. In every choice, there's an opportunity cost. If you decide to go to university, for example, you're giving up the income you could have earned by working full-time during those years plus whatever you could have purchased with the money used to attend school. You also may take on loans to pay for school, which will have to be paid back with future income that could have gone for other purposes.

The basics

While most people are aware of the direct costs of life - for example, when you take money out of your wallet to buy a cheeseburger - many ignore the indirect costs associated with those actions. These are the opportunity costs. At its core, an opportunity cost is what you lose by choosing one alternative over another.

Now, let's say you can choose between eating the aforementioned cheeseburger meal and putting £4.50 into savings. Each choice has benefits and drawbacks. If you choose the cheeseburger, you will likely have a nice lunch and a chance to leave the office. If you choose to save the money, you give up that break time and good food, but you get the chance to earn interest on that £4.50. That will give you more money in the future. Either way, you stand to gain and lose something. Every time you make a choice, you're weighing the opportunity cost of that action.

Opportunity costs extend beyond just the monetary costs of a decision, but it includes all real costs of making one choice over another, including the loss of time, energy and a derived pleasure/utility.

Using opportunity costs in our daily lives

For big choices like buying a home or starting a business, you may weigh the pros and cons, but generally, most of our day-to-day choices aren't made without a full understanding of the potential opportunity costs. If they're cautious about a purchase, most people just look at their savings account and check their balance before spending money. For the most part, we don't think about the things that we must give up when we make those decisions.

However, that kind of thinking could be dangerous. The problem lies when you never look at what else you could do with your money, or buy things blindly without considering the lost opportunities. Certainly, buying a cheeseburger for lunch occasionally can be a wise decision, especially if it gets you out of the office when your boss is throwing a fit. However, buying one cheeseburger every day for the next 25 years could lead to several missed opportunities. Aside from the potential harmful health effects of high cholesterol; investing that £4.50 could add up to just over £52,000 in that time frame, assuming a very doable rate of return of 5%.

This is just one simplistic example, but the basic message holds true for a variety of situations. From choosing whether to invest in "safe" treasury bonds or deciding to attend a public school over a private one, there are plenty of things to consider when making a decision in your personal finance life.

While it may sound like a bummer to have to think about opportunity costs every time you want to buy a candy bar or go on vacation, it's an important tool in order to make the best use of your money. When it comes to personal finance, you cannot go through your life on autopilot. There are unseen positives and negatives with each financial decision. However, the good news is that once you recognize that these costs exist, it becomes easier to make good personal finance choices.

Most people are aware of the seen costs when it comes to personal finance. We understand the direct costs for our actions. However, the unseen costs could be more important to realize. Understanding these opportunity costs is critical to making the best possible decisions with our money.

Rule #2

Never Put Your Wants Above Your Needs

Never put wants above needs is one of the most basic concepts of economics. This is all about Needs vs. Wants.

So what are they exactly?

A need is something you have to have, something you can't do without. A good example is food. If you don't eat, you won't survive for long. Many people have gone days without eating, but they eventually ate a lot of food. You might not need a whole lot of food, but you do need to eat.

A want is something you would like to have. It is not absolutely necessary, but it would be a good thing to have. A good example is music. Now, some people might argue that music is a need because they think they can't do without it, but you don't need music to survive, however, you do need to eat to survive.

These are general categories, of course. Some categories have both needs and wants. For instance, food could be a need or a want, depending on the type of food. You need to eat protein, vitamins, and minerals. How you get them is up to you (and your family). You can eat meat, nuts, or soy products to get protein. You can get fruits and vegetables to get vitamins and minerals. You can eat yogurt or cheese to get other vitamins and minerals. You can eat bread to get still more vitamins and minerals. These basic kinds of foods are needs.

Ice cream is a want. You don't really need to eat ice cream to survive. You can eat it to get some vitamins and minerals, but other foods like cheese and yogurt give you more of those same vitamins and minerals without giving you the fat that ice cream does. Still, ice cream tastes good to many people. They like to eat it. They want it, but they don't need it. They like it, but they don't have to have it to survive.

Alright, we've covered food. What other kinds of things does your body need to survive?

Another example is liquid. Your body has to have liquid to survive. Water is a good liquid to drink because it keeps you healthy. Milk and fruit juice are also good because they give you vitamins and minerals your body needs without giving you the fat and excess sugar found in cola. Still, cola tastes good. Drink a Pepsi or Coke or Mountain Dew or Sprite and you feel good because it tastes good. However, you don't need that cola to survive.

Our actual needs are pretty limited: food, shelter, clothing, companionship. Just about everything else is a "want," and our wants are essentially endless because our resources are limited, we have to make choices about which wants to fulfil. Also, the way we fulfil our needs involves a lot of choice. Shelter, for example, can be a bed at a mission for the homeless or a £120 million mansion. Our food choices offer a similar range, from beans and tap water consumed at home to steak and Dom Perignon at an exclusive restaurant. I've discovered many people believe they have to spend money in certain ways or in certain amounts, when in reality their spending is a choice -- or is at least based on choices they made earlier. If you're facing a monster mortgage payment, for example, it's because you chose to buy that home and selected that particular mortgage. Taking responsibility for our choices can be scary, but it should also be empowering. After all, if you have choices, you're not just a victim of circumstance.

Rule #3

Talk About Money and Be Honest

I was afraid to talk about money – and it cost me. I avoided talking about money for years and instead watched my financial situation spiral downwards. When I realised I had to talk about it, I still kept putting it off.

Important Things to Consider When Talking About Money

What is unresolved?
Look around your life, particularly your closest family and friends. In each of those relationships, there are likely things that are left unresolved, things that, in your perfect world, they would be resolved. Here are some examples.

Your partner.
Are you sharing the same dreams for the future? Do you have any debts that you're hiding? Are you in better – or worse – financial shape than your partner might believe? Are you in agreement about how to handle your respective property in the event of the other's passing? Is your relationship fulfilling you, making you happy?

Your parents.
Do they have an estate plan in place? A will, at least? Are they prepared for the financial costs of retirement? What are they expecting from you when they retire?

Your children.
Are they expecting you to pay for university? Are you expecting to? Are they expecting you to help with a wedding? Are you expecting to? Do they understand your estate planning?

Other relatives.
Do they owe you money? Do you owe them money? Are there other problems, such as caring for older family members? Who's responsible for what?

Your close friends.
Are they constantly engaging you in activities that cost more than you are comfortable spending? Do they owe you money? Do you owe them money? This is just a start. Even in my own life, after lots of talking about money with the people around me, I still don't feel as though the door is shut on all of these issues. I will say this, though: every time I made an effort to actually talk through these issues with someone important to me, I found that I had put it off for too long and worried about it too much, because it went easier than I expected and there was much relief afterwards.

Is everyone involved that should be?
Whenever you address a complex issue, the ramifications often affect all sorts of people, and it's usually a very poor idea to start making big changes without seeking their input.

So, before you even start discussing these things, get everyone involved that should be. If you're talking about a person's estate, make sure anyone who has a significant stake is involved in the discussion – or is at least carefully considered to be a part of the discussion.

Quite often, this seems painful. I immediately think of some of the estate planning situations I've witnessed and been involved with. It was obvious at times that things – and people – were being cut out in order to preserve the comfort of now while postponing the painful part until later.

Each time, it ended in disaster. Siblings not speaking to each other for the rest of their lives. Friendships ended because of "backstabbing" lawsuits.

You're better off swallowing your pride and getting everyone relevant to sit down and talk about things. If someone won't participate, that's their decision, but the door needs to be very open to them – and it needs to be clear that the door is open to them.

Getting the necessary information
Data is the enemy of lies, lies are the enemies of trusting relationships, and the maintenance of trusting relationships is why you're doing this in the first place.

Yes, people are defensive. Yes, it hurts to tell the whole truth sometimes. So make it easier on everyone – bring as much real data to the table as possible. Get out those statements and figure out how much there is.

People are going to be uncomfortable with this. The best thing you can do to quell that is to step up to the plate yourself. Bring your information and offer to show it. Your openness and honesty creates a standard that others will feel some strong desire to live up to, lest they look as though they are being dishonest or are hiding something.

What about feelings? Again, honesty is the best policy and, again, your best bet is to lead by example. Behave in exactly the way you'd like others involved to behave. Share every drop of your relevant information. State your opinions and feelings openly, honestly, and calmly.

Real information and real honesty are powerful tools for cutting through the layers of personal feelings and getting directly to the heart of the matter.

Getting it done
You know what you want to talk about. You're prepared to bring honesty to the table. You know who needs to be involved. Now, you just need to do it.

Plan to talk about it in a place that's as safe as possible for all of the participants – a comfortable place. A person's home is usually the best choice unless it inherently causes some discomfort.

It should also be a place where, if numbers are going to have to be analyzed, all of that data is easily available. Thus, if you're going to walk through some estate planning, you may want to do it at the home of the person whose estate is being planned.

You should schedule a very clear time when this is going to be discussed and make that time and date known to everyone who might be involved. Give plenty of time for this, so that you can schedule around any conflicts. Don't just decide one Saturday morning that everyone is going to meet that afternoon.

Another key factor: if it's really involved, plan things around another activity. Make dinner during the discussion so you can dine together afterwards – or dine as a break.

A final key factor: make sure that the meeting ends with some very clear actions for some or all of the people to take. What needs to be done to make these plans a reality? Without specific actions, nothing will actually happen as a result of the talk.

Dealing with Anger or Hurt Feelings

Money has such a huge emotional factor, you can pretty much expect that if a discussion is intense enough, people are going to get angry or upset or have some sort of emotional response. So, plan ahead for it.

1. Make a very clear rule that raising your voice or being obviously angry isn't allowed.

If someone gets angry, just call a time out and let everyone chill out. Nothing good comes from allowing a discussion to continue if participants are angry or upset because the emotion will just rapidly escalate. Then follow that rule. If someone gets upset, just take a break until everyone is calm again.

2. Make it clear to everyone what the end goal is and make sure you all agree.

If it's about estate planning, for example, make it clear that the goal is to help your parents develop a plan that reflects their wishes – and that their wishes are final because it's their estate.

3. Don't let hard feelings run after the event.

If you're sure that emotions are going to run high, plan a family dinner or other special event immediately afterwards to work on healing those stressed bonds. Feelings like these should not be allowed to fester.

Following Up

After the conversation, you'll likely find yourself with a list of actions and probably some bruised feelings. Both elements deserve some follow-up.

Talk to the people involved afterwards and see what you can do to alleviate any hurt feelings. Pull back to the general purpose of the meeting and remind them that the big goal actually happened, even if it hurt. Listen to their concerns and don't talk them down – agree with them, at least to the extent to let them know that their feelings are at least understood, even if you don't agree.

You should also follow up on any decided actions. Make sure that the people who agreed to do things actually do them. This might even involve some follow-up meetings to ensure that these actions happened or that further input is received.

This sounds like a lot of work but the benefits are tremendous: stronger relationships, an assurance that the important things are taken care of, and potential crises averted. Talking about money honestly is a huge positive once you get past one's fear of it.

Rule #4
Stop Trying To Impress Other People

This is a ticking time bomb and before you can effectively do this, you need to sit down and figure out the small handful of key values that are central in your life. Once you have figured out what those are, the rest is secondary – and that means you should seriously trim back your spending in those areas.

Stop trying to impress other people.

Warren Buffet is perhaps the quintessential example of the unimportance of impressing others. Being the second richest man on the planet affords him all the luxuries and toys he could ever dream up, yet he lives in the same house he's lived in for years, drives an older model car, and wears dated clothes. People who spend to impress typically have something within themselves that is lacking, and it's the 'impression' of success and importance that they need to fulfil that void. Being yourself is not only cheaper, but your life will be filled with a much better calibre of people as well, thereby enriching your life more than money or toys could ever afford.

If you buy a car that's flashy rather than focusing on one that gets the job done as efficiently as you can find, you're spending money to impress other people. If you go clothes shopping by the store sack full, you're spending money to impress other people. If you always have the latest gadget, you're spending money to impress other people. If you always must be seen at the coolest new place, you're spending money to impress other people.

Stop worrying about it.

I found it was really powerful for me to take people and split them into two groups: people whose opinions I cared about, and people whose opinions I didn't care about one way or another.

It was easy to stop caring about impressing people whose opinions I didn't care about. Who cares what they think? As long as I'm not doing something truly offensive or heinous – something that might potentially create a negative reputation for me – it doesn't matter what they think.

The trickier part was worrying about impressing other people whose opinions I do care about. People I want to meet – customers, friends, family, shouldn't I want to impress them?

Again, I go back to the basics. As long as I'm not offensive – meaning I'm clean, I'm presentable, and I behave myself – I don't need to impress these people with expensive, shiny things. The relationship I've built with them – or I'm going to build with them – is based on me, not on the material items. They'll either like me for me or they won't – no amount of shiny will change that.

So, to put it simply, take care of the basics. Have good hygiene. Keep yourself clean. Keep your weight under control. Wear reasonable clothing. Work on your communication skills. If you have them covered, you don't need to invest time and money into impressing other people. You will naturally connect with the people you need to connect with, and you won't connect with those you shouldn't connect with anyway.

Coming to this realization is incredibly valuable. It drops your clothing budget. It drops your automobile budget. It drops your electronics budget. It drops your housing budget. You don't need a McMansion, a shiny car, an iPhone, or a £50 haircut.

Yes, you may actually still want one or two of these things, but the impetus comes from what your personal core values are, not what other people around you seem to value or what marketing messages you receive.

For some people, it seems impossible. Their social cues come from advertising-laden media and from friends who also get their cues from advertising-laden media. They believe they need a slick cell phone and £200 casual clothes. Their self-worth revolves around that little burst they get from impressing others.

How to Break Free From Trying to Impress People

1. Take the lead.

Be a trendsetter within your group. Back away from the expenses and activities that revolve mostly around impressing other people. Make suggestions for activities that don't revolve around showing off.

2. Try new activities.

You can do this either with your circle of friends or on your own, but try out new things that you might never have considered before. Think of things that seemed fun to you but you never got involved with because others around you decried them – and you were trying hard to impress them by agreeing.

3. Guide the conversation.

If the conversation turns to bland compliments of each other and insults of people outside your group, steer the conversation away from it. Focus on being positive towards everyone, particularly in non-material areas. Pick areas you're passionate about (don't be a one trick pony – figure out several) and guide the conversation there instead.

4. Use your compliments wisely.

Offer compliments on jobs well done, but don't bother with big compliments on new gadgets or new clothing or a shiny new car. It'll become clear that what you value are people who take charge of their life, not people who fritter away their money trying to impress others.

5. Share personal growth oriented thoughts.

Instead of talking about popular culture and "stuff" all the time, instead mix in some thoughts on personal growth. Talk about ways you're trimming your spending in positive ways. Talk about your big aspirations and dreams. Encourage others to share theirs as well. It also helps to read good materials in these areas so that you have more food for your own thought and more ideas to share.

6. Explore new relationships.

If your circle of friends is still focused too heavily on impressing others and on material gains, spend some time exploring new relationships. Call up people you've thought of as interesting but simply wouldn't fit in your old group and see what they're up to. Connect with people at the new activities you're trying. There will be more on this in 'Rule #14.'

In short, don't play socially by the tired old rules that revolve around needing to impress people. Instead, spend your time on things that bring real value to you – and give real value to others.

Rule #5

Spend Less Than You Earn

Spend less than you earn sounds so simple, doesn't it? Yet there are many people out there burying themselves in debt (spending more than they earn) or living purely salary to salary (spending exactly what they earn).

WHAT DO YOU GAIN BY SPENDING LESS THAN YOU EARN?

1. You start getting rid of your debts.

Spending less than you earn releases up the money you need to make larger payments on your debts. Over time, they begin to disappear, reducing your monthly bills and giving you even more breathing room.

2. You start saving.

First, you build up some cash savings in your savings account, enabling you to roll through emergencies (like a car breakdown or a job loss). You'll also have the breathing room to start saving for retirement, paving yourself a great future for your golden years.

3. Your stress level plummets.

Having knowledge that you have fewer debts, your emergencies are covered, and your retirement is being planned for reduces your stress level. You sleep better, your overall health improves, and you feel happier about life.

4. You are able to explore possibilities previously unreachable.

When your debts are gone and you are spending far less than you're bringing in, you suddenly have many more career possibilities. You don't have to stick with your high-stress job – you have the financial freedom to move on and pursue your dreams. You can live where – and how – you want to live.

All of that comes back to one basic principle – **spend less than you earn.**

However, this statement actually has two parts.

Spend less refers to the fact that you do need to cut your spending. The first step doesn't need to be anything drastic – nor should it be. Many of the more extreme money-saving tips come from people who have already tried out the basic tips and love them, so they seek out more intense strategies to further cut their spending. I do this myself – I'm always trying out new money-saving strategies, discarding the ones that don't work for me and keeping the ones that do.

ARE YOU READY TO SPENDING LESS?

1. Go through every monthly required bill.

Ask yourself 'do I really need that service'? Do you really use Netflix enough, or could you just rent a movie once in a while? Do you really use your cell phone much at all, or could you just replace it with a pay-as-you-go phone? Then, go through each bill and see if there are any optional services you can eliminate. Do you really need premium cable? Do you really need unlimited text messages?

2. Keep diligent track of your spending.

Keep a notebook in your pocket and write down every expense you have. The simple process of doing this will make you think twice about unnecessary expenses. When you do have a month's worth of expenses written down, take a careful look at them. Ask yourself whether or not each of these expenses actually contributed to the value and joy of your life. That process will offer a lot of insight for you as to where your spending is going to waste.

3. Monitor your routines.

Watch what you do every day (or most days). Are there things you do each day that cost money? Those things are the most powerful ones to adjust, as trimming just £1 from your daily spending saves you £365 a year. Do you stop at a coffee shop each day? Why not cut down your daily order a bit, or switch to a different shop, or start making your coffee at home? Do you eat out every day? Perhaps you can start brown bagging it a few days a week. Look at every regular expense you have.

4. Switch bank accounts.

The vast majority of people are with banks that don't treat

them very well. No interest at all on their current account; loads of fees for Automated Teller Machine (ATM) use; draconian overdraft policies; little interest rate on savings accounts; monthly usage fees of all kinds. All of these things are a waste of money. Switch your accounts to a bank that respects you.

4. Do some one-time energy improvements around your home.

Replace some of your light bulbs with energy-saving light bulbs and LEDs. Install a programmable thermostat. Air-seal your home. Blanket your water heater. Install some Smart Strips to cut down on electricity use. These tactics will cut down your energy bill significantly, directly reducing your bills.

The rest of the phrase, than you earn, though, points to the other part of the equation: increasing your earnings. Increasing your earnings gives you more money with which to get rid of your debts, save for your big dreams, and build a foundation for whatever future moves you may want to make.

There are countless ways to earn more money, but there are several tactics almost anyone can apply in their life.

WAYS TO START INCREASING YOUR INCOME

1. Don't waste time at work.

The time you spend sitting idle, watching television, browsing the web, or chatting on IM or Twitter with your buddies is time you've effectively lost. Instead, invest that time in something devoted to your career, even if it's not directly on a work project. There are lots of things you can always be working on – see the other things below, for example.

2. Work on your transferable skills.
I'm a big believer in transferable skills – skills that one can utilize in almost any career path. Work on mastering such skills. Jump on any and all opportunities to speak in public. Hammer out an effective time management scheme for you. Get into a routine of organizing and filing your paperwork. Brainstorm ideas for things going on in your office. Write clear documentation for the standard procedures of your work. Step up to the plate, take charge of a work project, and get the ball moving forward. All of these things push you towards developing skills that are genuinely useful no matter where you're heading in life.

3. Build strong relationships with as many people in your field.

Join social networks like Twitter or LinkedIn and start conversations with people in your career. Send emails to people you've interacted with a lot in your career and keep up with what they're doing. If you have an opportunity to connect people that can help each other, do it immediately, without hesitation. Share what you know and be valuable to others.

4. Start a side business.

I don't mean filling out surveys or other things you can use to burn a few minutes during the commercial breaks on 'Big Brother' and earn a few pennies. I mean actually devote serious time and effort to turning a passion you have into a money-making enterprise. What do you love doing that can bring you extra income? Whether it is blogging, video-blogging, auto-detailing, baking, buying and selling on eBay, find something you love and turn it into a business.

Keep that rule in mind: spend less than you earn. Each move you make to maximize the gap between what you earn and what you spend will put you in a better place in your life.

Rule #6

Plan Ahead Before You Spend

W̲henever some people see statements like 'plan ahead before you spend', they roll their eyes. "Your life must be boring if you have to plan ahead every time you spend" is a typical refrain.

The big problem with that thinking is that it makes an incredibly false substitution. Planning ahead does not mean the elimination of spontaneity in life; in fact, once you get into the routine, it can often feel more spontaneous because unplanned chaotic spontaneity is no longer the norm.

Also, it's that unplanned chaotic spontaneity that gets people in deep spending trouble.

It's easy to apply the principle of planning ahead every time you spend for the big purchases. For most of us, saving and planning for houses and cars and vacations is completely normal and reasonable behaviour. We don't want to go on a vacation that costs thousands of pounds without some planning, after all, and we certainly see the logic in planning for such purchases.

Where this begins to break down for many people is when the purchases get smaller. A cell phone plan might get some research from some, or it might be completely impulsive, even though fifteen minutes of online research can save you hundreds a year. Christmas gifts are often bought in minimal time, even though you can often find better gifts for the same price or better deals on the gifts you bought with just a bit of footwork and planning. These things add up – the ten minutes spent planning for such a purchase might net you £50 in savings, which is well worth it for many people.

For purchases more than £100 or so (over their lifetime), just spend five minutes making sure you're getting a good deal and that you can adequately and easily afford the item. If you're convinced, use the thirty day rule. Put that purchase on hold for thirty days. If you still want it after thirty days and you can afford it, go for it.

Where the idea of planning ahead really breaks down, though, is with the small impulse buy like dinner at a local restaurant, a movie, a new DVD at the store, a new shirt, a new pair of trousers, a ticket to a football game.

Quite often, these items are bought quickly with almost no forethought. Sure, it can be fun to do something spontaneously, but that spontaneity can drown you.

Let's say you go shopping with a friend. On a whim, you buy a new dress, and then the two of you go out to dinner together and head out to a movie. For many people, this is a nice, fun evening.

The worrisome side of it comes later. You go home, look through your credit card statements, and realize that the £50 you spent that night (previously unaccounted for) has now completely tapped you out. You haven't got enough money to cover the electric bill. So you pay it late – and there's a late fee on next month's bill. However, by then you've moved on to another completely unplanned expense.

Variety and spontaneity are two of the spices of life, but it's foolish to let those spices cost you more than they should.

Instead, plan ahead a little for those spontaneous moments. Each month, put £100 in cash in your wallet and let that be your "spontaneous" money for the month. You can do whatever you want with it and it's fine because you planned for that amount. An impromptu moment doesn't mean that you're going to be late on a bill at all.

When that £100 is gone, it's gone but don't worry, it's no big deal, just wait until the calendar turns and you can refuel.

Obviously, you can adjust that amount to whatever you'd like – more in some situations, less in others. The reason for doing it is simple: **it allows you to be spontaneous without being destructively chaotic with your finances.**

Some people might wisely see this as the rudiments of a budget – and they're right. This is simple budgeting at its finest. By putting that cash in your wallet, you're assigning an amount to your spontaneous spending. The amount that remains in your current account is handled differently – you pay your bills and your savings with it. One big danger when people follow this idea: they put their £100 in their wallet and then find it's gone by the ninth of the month. Then they spend twenty one days miserable, thinking that this plan is stupid or talking themselves into getting more out of their current account.

Don't live out the month. Then, sit down at the end of the month and take a serious look at the month as a whole. Did you give up anything vital during those twenty one days? Did you do anything during those nine days that didn't really add any value to your life?

You might find that by taking a real look at your spontaneous spending that you're doing things that you don't really find valuable. The next month that money might hold out until the twenty seventh of the month simply because you're a bit more selective in what you do with your mad money – and there's no adverse effect on your happiness at all.

After a few months, you might find an adjustment is in order – either up or down. Such an adjustment is fine as long as you're paying all your bills and either actively reducing your debt or increasing your personal savings.

The real key is this: every action you take is worthy of a bit of thought, either beforehand, in the moment, or afterwards. A bit of reflection often tells you whether that choice was right or wrong for you – whether it actually adds value to your life.

Then, taking the conscious steps to reduce those things that don't add much value becomes easy – you just eliminate the negative and by default the positive in your life is accentuated.

Yes, for some people, a simple budget can be incredibly useful but for many others, just a bit of planning ahead can make the big difference that they need.

Rule #7

Open An Emergency Fund

T he first step along the way is to understand what an emergency fund actually is. An emergency fund is cash that you've saved up for the sole purpose of helping you maintain your normal life through the emergencies that life hands you. Most of the time, you shouldn't touch the emergency fund at all – it just sits there earning a bit of interest and waiting until you actually need it; when you lose your job; when an appliance breaks down; or when your car needs a repair.

Quite often, people who don't have an emergency fund see the idea of having to save up money as some form of punishment – after all, money put in a savings account and locked away is money that can't be used to live, right?

Actually, it's quite the opposite – having an emergency fund means that you do have room to breathe. You don't have to completely panic if your car breaks down or if you lose your job or if you suddenly need to replace a hot water heater. Instead of having to find some way to squeeze those expenses onto a credit card or beg a friend for some money to help, you can just pay the bill – no worries.

Another problem that I often hear when it comes to emergency funds is the temptation that people have to spend the money on things that aren't emergencies. They see that they've built up several hundred pounds in savings and they start thinking about buying a flat panel television or going on a trip – and that's just what they do.

If you want to have a savings account for big splurges, that's great – start a "splurge fund," too, if it makes sense for you. It's important, though, to just leave the emergency fund completely alone until you need it. Deposit money in there and don't even look at the balance until an actual emergency occurs.

First Steps with Emergency Funds

Set your initial target low

So, what's the first step? Many people bite off a gigantic goal for their emergency fund right off the bat and then find that it's very hard to get there. Eight months of living expenses is an enormous goal, one that will take years to reach – and along the way, you're bound to get disheartened.

Instead, one great way to start is to set a goal that's more reasonable. Make it your initial goal to have an emergency fund of just £250 or £500. That's a goal that you can reach in just a few months (or even less if you're in a good income situation) and yet it's an amount that can make a huge difference when you have an emergency.

Then, break that goal down into smaller pieces. Perhaps you can save £25 a week. If that's the case, you can have a £250 emergency fund in just ten weeks, so you can set that as your overall goal. Maybe you can put away £40 a week, which would bring you to the £500 goal in three months.

My advice is not to set your savings plan too high at first, either in terms of the amount you can save each week or the overall amount. It should challenge you just a bit, but not be a number that's simply unreachable.

Find your breathing room

"That's great," you're thinking, "but where am I going to come up with £25 a week? I barely make ends meet now."

That's a pretty typical sentiment from people who are just beginning to turn their financial situation around. There are a lot of ways to come up with extra money throughout the month.

Request a rate reduction on your credit cards

If you're carrying a credit card balance, getting your interest rate reduced will directly save you money each month. Just flip over your credit card, call the number on the back, ask to speak to a supervisor, and simply request that the rate be reduced. Suggest that you're considering transferring your balance off of the card.

Shop around for better car insurance and homeowners insurance

According to an annual survey of Consumer Reports readers, many folks have stayed with the same car insurer for 15 years. The insurance industry says this is a good thing. Some say that, if you stay with the same carrier for several years, you may receive a discount for being a long-term policyholder, but that may not always be best. Insurance companies can change their appetite for risk and their pricing over time. Depending on your profile and where you live, you might be able to save hundreds of pounds by shopping around every few years and asking for discounts.

If you haven't compared costs for your car and home insurance in awhile, start with 'Compare the market', 'Go Compare', 'Confused', websites for starters. Just visit their websites, get some quotes, and make a switch.

Install a programmable thermostat – and program it

Pretty simple, actually – it just takes thirty minutes or so and will cut your cooling and heating bill by 20 or 30 percent. Set it so that the air conditioner and/or furnace don't run while you're sleeping or at work so that the energy isn't wasted when no one is around or awake to enjoy it.

Use a list for grocery shopping

Ten minutes of planning before you go will save you at least ten minutes in the store, plus it will help you stay focused on the stuff you actually need, reducing your grocery bill because you're putting less unnecessary stuff in the cart.

Transform one splurge a month

Instead of going out for an expensive dinner once a month, turn that dinner into a meal prepared at home. You'll save quite a bit even if you prepare something very fancy in your own kitchen.

Set up a carpool

Find someone that lives fairly close to you that works where you do and start carpooling together. Even if you can only do it a few days a week, you'll still drastically cut down on your commute costs, plus it will be a lot harder to stop for those impulse splurges.

Use public transportation

Even better than driving, get in the habit of using public transportation for your commuting needs. Most metropolitan areas have surprisingly good public transportation options – and they're far cheaper (and not all that much more time consuming) than driving yourself.

Get on the bicycle

Want to start getting in better shape? Only live a mile or two from your work? That's a perfect situation to get a bicycle and start using it for the commute instead of wasting your pounds on fuel and car maintenance.

Trim unnecessary monthly bills

Are you subscribing to Netflix but rarely using it? Cut it! Are you paying for premium cable channels that you never watch? Trim them!

Snowflake

Quite often, when people come into a bit of unexpected money, they tend to spend it without thinking about it. They decide not to stop for coffee, but then choose to spend it later on take out, for example. Instead of spending that "found money," take some or all of it and immediately put it into your emergency fund. If you have online banking, that's pretty easy – just transfer it out of your current account.

The key thing here is to actually save this savings. Instead of just spending the money on something else, put that money away towards your emergency fund. If you find that you're actually saving more than £50 a week with these tactics, then put more into the emergency fund or increase the amount you're putting into your retirement savings.

Make it automatic

So, you've trimmed £50 a week from your spending, but now you have this cash sitting there and it's tempting to spend it on something more exciting than an emergency fund. You're tempted...

... but you don't have to be tempted. Instead, you can set up an automatic savings plan to sweep that money straight out of your current account and into your savings account that you're using for an emergency fund.

If you haven't already, I recommend setting up an online savings account at a bank separate than the one you normally do business with for your emergency fund. Doing this not only lets you shop around for a bank with good service and good savings account rates, but it also causes you to put the money in a place that's not quite so easy to access. You can't just run to the ATM or stop by the teller window and withdraw cash from it – you have to go to your computer, order a transfer, and wait for a day or two to access the cash, which is more than enough time for you to think carefully about what you're doing and not get sucked in by impulse.

So, sign up for an online savings account with good service and a solid interest rate, set up an automatic plan at that bank to sweep £50 (or whatever you can save) a week into that savings account, and then forget about it. Since you've already freed up that money through tightening your belt just a bit, this should be quite easy to do.

Set reasonable milestones along the way

In a few months, you'll hit that first milestone – and it'll feel good. That account will have enough money in it that it'll start earning a bit of interest on its own and you'll start to feel in control of the situation.

Now is the time to keep going. Set another goal – an emergency fund of £1,000. Keep that automatic savings plan in place.

Once you reach that goal, aim for a single month's worth of living expenses. Then two months. Then three. And just keep watching that emergency fund grow.

Obviously, when you do have an emergency, tap that fund. Don't put your car repair bill on the credit card. Don't start living on plastic while you're between jobs. Instead, keep living a financially stable life thanks to your planning ahead.

You might just find that this is a lot of fun – so you might start seeking out more ways to save. Just keep setting goals for yourself and keep pushing yourself just a little to make it there.

Before you know it, your life won't be disrupted by these kinds of emergencies – and you'll sleep a lot better at night knowing that.

Rule #8

Eliminate (And Avoid) High Interest Debt

This rule is about as subtle as a sledgehammer, of course. High interest debt is a terrible idea, and even low interest debts are a terrible idea. Let's count the ways.

REASONS TO AVOID HIGH INTEREST DEBT

The higher the interest rate, the more money you lose.

Leave a £1,000 debt on a credit card with a 5.5% APR for a year and you lose £55 – not good. However, if you bump that amount up to a level that's typical for credit cards – say, 19.9% – and you're up to £199 a year. Gone. Poof. Vanished.

The higher the debt level, the more money you lose.

So, you have £1,000 debt on a credit card with a 19.9% APR and you lose £199 a year. Bump that up to £5,000 and you're losing £998 a year with nothing in return.

You're open to extra fees

Late payment fees, over-limit fees, annual fees, ATM fees, cash advance fees — are all hidden fees that drain your money. If there's a way to ding you, credit card companies will figure out how to do it. A fee here, a fee there, and you're suddenly watching even more money evaporate for nothing in return.

A required debt payment each month reduces your freedom.

With that £5,000 debt above, you're paying about £100 every single month as a minimum payment. That's £100 you could be saving for a down payment. That's £100 you could be saving to start a business. That's £100 you could be saving for a car. That's £100 you could be saving towards retiring early. That's £100 you could be saving towards a great vacation. Your freedom is gone, eaten by the debt monster.

High interest debt brings other debt into your life.

You make a big commitment to getting rid of all of this debt, then start really bearing down on it. You get half of the debt gone, and then all of a sudden disaster strikes. You lose your job. Your car breaks down. Your hot water heater leaks water all over the basement. Suddenly, you're busting out the plastic again to take care of the problem – and you're right back deep into debt. It's like escaping from quicksand – if all of your strokes are perfect, you can pull yourself out slowly, but if even one little thing goes wrong, you're slurped right back in. In other words, it costs you money, costs you freedom, and puts you into a vicious cycle of even more debt.

How to Eliminate High Interest Debt

There are really two prongs to getting out of this trap. Whether you're avoiding it entirely or you're trying to escape from the pit of despair, there's one big first step you must take.

Build a small emergency fund

The first step is not paying off debt. Paying off debt first is like kicking to get out of quicksand without getting your arms around something safe first – you might be able to kick out, but if anything goes wrong, you'll just be sucked in deeper.

So, no matter what state you're in, give yourself that rock – a cash emergency fund, sitting in a savings account. It doesn't need to be too big – £1,000 should be your big target, but just starts by putting £20 a week into savings – or more if you can swing it. Instruct your bank to do this automatically. Do it right now – call up your bank and ask them to do it.

You won't miss that £20 a week. Your life will quickly find little ways to save – you'll eat a few less expensive meals, start carpooling with a friend, or skip a few coffee shop visits and you're there. What happens is that over the course of three months, your savings account reaches £250. After just shy of a year, your savings account will have £1,000 in it.

If you're already making extra payments on your debts and you don't have an emergency fund, stop those overpayments for a while and deposit that extra amount into your savings each month until you reach that £1,000.

Leave this money alone except for an emergency. You

might be tempted to spend it on something fun or to pay off a big slug of debt with it. Don't. That money is your rock – it'll be there for you if your car breaks down or you lose your job. You won't be sucked back into debt by these unfortunate events – your savings will save you.

What do you do when you reach that £1,000 level? Many people keep saving. Then, once a month, they sweep anything over £1,000 back into their checking and use it to make an extra debt payment, knocking down their debt without touching their £1,000 emergency fund.

Here's the big key: if you do face that emergency, like having your car break down or losing your job and you tap that emergency fund, replenish the fund after the emergency. Go back to minimum payments on your debts and rebuild that fund. It's your rock.

Make a debt repayment plan

When you have that emergency fund in place, it's time to start tackling your debts in an intelligent fashion. Make a big list of all of your debts; then, attempt to get the rate on each of those debts reduced. Give your credit card companies a call and negotiate your rate down. Contact your local credit union and see if there are any opportunities to consolidate your debt at a lower rate.

Once you've done these things, list all of your remaining debts in order of interest rate, with the highest rate first. Then throw everything you can at the highest interest rate debt. Your only extra payment should be towards this top debt, and it should be the biggest overpayment you can muster without tapping your emergency fund - live lean. Sell off stuff you don't use. Find ways to earn a few extra bucks to throw at it.

Once that first debt is gone, throw everything at the next one, then the next one, then the next one. Your extra payments will grow larger because you've got fewer minimum payments to make, and soon you'll find yourself free.

Avoiding High Interest Debt

I'm not a "no debt" absolutist. I think that home mortgages are often worthwhile for most people, and I think credit cards can be a useful tool if used carefully.

Having said that, many people do not use credit cards carefully. Instead of carefully using them as a tool during very regular purchases (like fuel) and then setting the cash aside to pay the bill in full each month, they use credit cards mindlessly to buy whatever they throw in their shopping cart, not worrying too much about prices because, hey, the credit card will cover it!

Bad idea! If you have any inclination in that direction, cut up your credit cards, seriously. It's the equivalent of swinging a chainsaw around with your eyes closed after knocking back three shots – you might luck out and wind up safe, but it's more likely to wind up bloody and painful.

Instead, adopt a different approach. Leave your card at home most of the time. When you do use it, use it for specific purposes, like using a BP credit card and use it only at BP gas stations so you can get a nice kick back, or use the Target Visa only at Target to get 10% off your entire purchase regularly, and pay off the balance in full every time. Otherwise, leave it at home and use a debit card (one that features a Visa or MasterCard logo) for your purchases because then you're actually accountable for every dime you spend while still enjoying the convenience of card use.

There are two big reasons for using this approach instead of going entirely down the cash road. First, it builds a positive credit rating, and a good credit rating improves your insurance rates and helps your employment opportunities. Second, using cards only in a much targeted fashion – as shown above – and paying off the bills in full each time results in some sweet cash kickbacks – 3% at least.

You've just got to respect the tool – and not start swinging it around like a toddler with an axe.

Rule #9
Make Sure You Invest

O ne of the most compelling reasons for you to invest is the prospect of not having to work your entire life! Bottom line, there are only two ways to make money: by working and/or by having your assets work for you.

If you keep your money in your back pocket instead of investing it, your money doesn't work for you and you will never have more money than what you save. By investing your money, you are getting your money to generate more money by earning interest on what you put away or by buying and selling assets that increase in value.

It really doesn't matter how you do it. Whether you invest in stocks, bonds, mutual funds, options and futures, precious metals, real estate, your own small business, or any combination thereof, the objective is the same: to make investments that will generate more cash for you in the future. As they say, "Money isn't everything, but happiness alone can't keep out the rain."

Whether your goal is to send your children to university or to retire on a yacht in the Mediterranean, investing is essential to getting you where you want to be.

NOT SURE WHICH INVESTMENTS TO UNDERTAKE? DON'T WORRY ABOUT IT.

You're twenty five. You want to retire at age sixty,

so you've got thirty five years to go. You decide that £750,000 is a good target. So you start looking into investments.

You do a week's worth of research, pick an investment that seems pretty good and stable over the long haul, and you decide to dive in and start saving right then and there.

You start stashing away £5,000 a year, and that investment only has to earn 7% a year to get you to your goal. You don't have to have sleepless nights worrying about your investment – 7% is a pretty reasonable goal.

Now, let's say you look at them – and you're overwhelmed. You decide to wait a year – and that year becomes five.

You start stashing away £5,000 a year now, but the outlook is decidedly worse. You now have to earn 9% a year in order to make that £750,000 goal. Instead of being able to sock that money away and not worry about it, you'll now have to micromanage it – and even then, you likely still won't make it.

What's the moral of the story? **You're better off starting your savings now rather than waiting until you find the "perfect" investment.** The perfect is always the enemy of the good. Sure, you can keep your eye out for a better investment, but you don't have to have worldbeating Peter Lynch-like returns in order to make your goals.

Primary Objectives

The options for investing our savings are continually increasing, yet every single investment vehicle can be easily categorized according to three fundamental characteristics - safety, income and growth - which also correspond to types of investor objectives. While it is possible for an investor to have more than one of these objectives, the success of one must come at the expense of others. Let's examine these three types of objectives, the investments that are used to achieve them and the ways in which investors can incorporate them in devising a strategy.

Safety

Perhaps there is truth to the axiom that there is no such thing as a completely safe and secure investment. Yet we can get close to ultimate safety for our investment funds through the purchase of government-issued securities in stable economic systems, or through the purchase of the highest quality corporate bonds issued by the economy's top companies. Such securities are arguably the best means of preserving principal while receiving a specified rate of return.

The safest investments are usually found in the money market, which includes such securities as Treasury bills (T-bills), certificates of deposit (CD), commercial paper or bankers' acceptance slips, or in the fixed income (bond) market in the form of municipal and other government bonds, and in corporate bonds. The securities listed above are ordered according to the typical spectrum of increasing risk and, in turn, increasing potential yield. To compensate for their higher risk, corporate bonds return a greater yield than T-bills.

It is important to realize that there's an enormous range of relative risk within the bond market. At one end are government and high-grade corporate bonds, which are considered some of the safest investments around; at the other end are junk bonds, which have a lower investment grade and may have more risk than some of the more speculative stocks. In other words, it's incorrect to think that corporate bonds are always safe, but most instruments from the money market can be considered very safe.

Income

The safest investments are also the ones that are likely to have the lowest rate of income return or yield. Investors must inevitably sacrifice a degree of safety if they want to increase their yields. This is the inverse relationship between safety and yield: as yield increases, safety generally goes down and vice versa.

In order to increase their rate of investment return and

take on risk above that of money market instruments or government bonds, investors may choose to purchase corporate bonds or preferred shares with lower investment ratings. Investment grade bonds rated at A or AA are slightly riskier than AAA bonds, but presumably also offer a higher income return than AAA bonds. Similarly, BBB rated bonds can be thought to carry medium risk but offer less potential income than junk bonds, which offer the highest potential bond yields available but at the highest possible risk. Junk bonds are the most likely to default.

Most investors, even the most conservative-minded ones, want some level of income generation in their portfolios, even if it's just to keep up with the economy's rate of inflation. However, maximizing income return can be an overarching principle for a portfolio, especially for individuals who require a fixed sum from their portfolio every month. A retired person who requires a certain amount of money every month is well served by holding reasonably safe assets that provide funds over and above other income-generating assets, such as pension plans, for example.

Growth of capital

This discussion has thus far been concerned only with safety and yield as investing objectives, and has not considered the potential of other assets to provide a rate of return from an increase in value, often referred to as a capital gain. Capital gains are entirely different from yield in that they are only realized when the security is sold for a price that is higher than the price at which it was originally purchased. Selling at a lower price is referred to as a capital loss. Therefore, investors seeking capital gains are likely not those who need a fixed, ongoing source of investment returns from their portfolio, but rather those who seek the possibility of longer-term growth.

Growth of capital is most closely associated with the purchase of common stock, particularly growth securities, which offer low yields but considerable opportunity for increase in value. For this reason, common stock generally ranks among the most speculative of investments as their return depends on what will happen in an unpredictable future. Blue-chip stocks, by contrast, can potentially offer the best of all worlds by possessing reasonable safety, modest income and potential for growth in capital generated by long-term increases in corporate revenues and earnings as the company matures. Yet rarely is any common stock able to provide the near-absolute safety and income-generation of government bonds.

It is also important to note that capital gains offer potential tax advantages by virtue of their lower tax rate in most jurisdictions. Funds that are garnered through common stock offerings, for example, are often geared toward the growth plans of small companies, a process that is extremely important for the growth of the overall economy. In order to encourage investments in these areas, governments choose to tax capital gains at a lower rate than income. Such systems serve to encourage entrepreneurship and the founding of new businesses that help the economy grow.

Secondary Objectives

Tax minimization

An investor may pursue certain investments in order to adopt tax minimization as part of his or her investment strategy. A highly-paid executive, for example, may want to seek investments with favourable tax treatment in order to lessen his or her overall income tax burden. Making contributions to an ISA or other tax-sheltered retirement plan, such as a private pension, can be an effective tax minimization strategy.

Marketability / liquidity

Many of the investments we have discussed are reasonably illiquid, which means they cannot be immediately sold and easily converted into cash. Achieving a degree of liquidity, however, requires the sacrifice of a certain level of income or potential for capital gains.

Common stock is often considered the most liquid of investments, since it can usually be sold within a day or two of the decision to sell. Bonds can also be fairly marketable, but some bonds are highly illiquid, or non-tradable, possessing a fixed term. Similarly, money market instruments may only be redeemable at the precise date at which the fixed term ends. If an investor seeks liquidity, money market assets and non-tradable bonds aren't likely to be held in his or her portfolio. As we have seen from each of the five objectives discussed above, the advantages of one often comes at the expense of the benefits of another. If an investor desires growth, for instance, he or she must often sacrifice some income and safety. Therefore, most portfolios will be guided by one pre-eminent objective, with all other potential objectives occupying less significant weight in the overall scheme.

Choosing a single strategic objective and assigning weightings to all other possible objectives is a process that depends on such factors as the investor's temperament, his or her stage of life, marital status, family situation and so forth. Out of the multitude of possibilities out there, each investor is sure to find an appropriate mix of investment opportunities. You need only be concerned with spending the appropriate amount of time and effort in finding, studying and deciding on the opportunities that match your objectives.

Rule #10
Stop Wasting Time

Whether we assign a pound value to it or not, time is valuable to us. Think about it: How much of your typical work week do you spend stressed about not having enough time to complete a task or reach a goal?

There are lots of different ways to tackle the issue of time management — you can download apps, adjust your sleep time, create lists, etc. But if you don't fully understand why it's important for you to better manage your time, those apps and lists aren't going to help you. If you don't have the motivation to use them, you won't.

You have to first look at the big picture. Get a handle on why managing your time effectively is important, and what you stand to gain from it.

You can get started by reviewing these 8 reasons time management is crucial:

1.   Time is limited.

No matter how you slice it, there are only 24 hours in a day. That applies to you, and to your co-worker who only seems able to do half the amount of work you do. But it also applies to the former co-worker who consistently accomplishes more than you, and was promoted as a result. If you want to rise through the ranks, you have to acknowledge the importance of finding a way to manage this limited resource.

2. You can accomplish more with less effort.

When you learn to take control of your time, you improve your ability to focus. And with increased focus comes enhanced efficiency, because you don't lose momentum. You'll start to breeze through tasks more quickly (the workday will also seem to fly by).

3. Improved decision-making ability.

Whether you rely on a time-chunking technique or discover the power of list-making, you'll soon find that a nice side benefit of good time management skills is the ability to make better decisions. When you feel pressed for time and have to make a decision, you're more likely to jump to conclusions without fully considering every option. That leads to poor decision making.

Through effective time management, you can eliminate the pressure that comes from feeling like you don't have enough time. You'll start to feel more calm and in control. When the time comes to examine options and make a decision, instead of rushing through the process, you can take time to carefully consider each option, and when you're able to do that, you diminish your chances of making a bad decision.

4. Become more successful in your career.

Time management is the key to success. It allows you to

take control of your life rather than following the flow of others. As you accomplish more each day, make more sound decisions, and feel more in control, people notice. Leaders in your business will come to you when they need to get things done. And that increased exposure helps put you in line for advancement opportunities.

5. **Learning opportunities are everywhere.**
Obviously, the more you learn the more valuable you are to your employer. Plus great learning opportunities are around you, if you've got time to stop and take advantage them.

When you work more efficiently, you have that time. You can help out with that new product launch your development team's been working on. Volunteer to help host your company's open house. Even just enjoying a nice lunch with teammates in other departments can prove eye-opening.

The more you learn about your company and your industry, the better your chances of making a positive impression.

6. **Reduce stress.**

When you don't have control of your time, it's easy to end up feeling rushed and overwhelmed; and when that happens, it can be hard to figure out how long it's going to take to complete a task. Think of a time when you were about to miss a deadline and were frantically trying to finish the project. If someone dumped a surprise on your desk at that moment and asked you how long it would take to finish the surprise task, how could you even begin to answer their question?

Once you learn how to manage your time, you no longer subject yourself to that level of stress. Besides it being better for your health, you have a clearer picture of the demands on your time. You're better able to estimate how long a given task will take you to complete, and you know you can meet the deadline.

7.   **Free time is necessary.**

Everyone needs time to relax and unwind. Unfortunately, though, many of us don't get enough of it. Between jobs, family responsibilities, errands, and upkeep on the house and the yard, most of us are hard-pressed to find even 10 minutes to sit and do nothing.

Having good time management skills helps you find that time. When you're busy, you're getting more done. You accumulate extra time throughout your day that you can use later to relax, unwind, and prepare for a good night's sleep.

8. Self-discipline is valuable

When you practice good time management, you leave no room for procrastination. The better you get at it, the more self-discipline you learn. This is a valuable skill that will begin to impact other areas of your life where a lack of discipline has kept you from achieving a goal.

THE POSITIVE CYCLE OF GOOD TIME MANAGEMENT

Looking through the list above, it's easy to see the multiplicative effect of time management. Good time management allows you to accomplish more in a shorter period of time, which leads to more free time, which lets you take advantage of learning opportunities, lowers your stress, and helps you focus, which leads to more career success. Each benefit of time management improves another aspect of your life. All you have to do is get the cycle started.

Whenever we find ourselves wasting time, we take directly away from those precious hours. We get behind at work, reducing our ability to earn more and thus taking away from the enjoyment of that time or the safety of it. We waste idle time at home and then when something truly worthwhile comes along, we can't participate – we have too many other things we're behind on.

To put it simply, wasting time takes away from those valuable hours that we work so hard for. It strips away their quality and it strips away their safety. Time management simply seeks to give us more of those hours – or to make the other hours produce more money.

Here's an example. Some days, when I sit down to work, I make the decision to dive right in. I've got some big idea on my mind and I can't wait to research it or plan out how I might use it. So I'll rip through most of an article in thirty minutes or so – and then find myself at a dead end. Where am I going with this? I idle for a bit, and then eventually delete the article. I've wasted forty minutes.

On another day, I'll start off by making a list of all of the things I need to accomplish for the day. I'll decide what posts I'm going to write and list the main idea of each one. Then I'll take each of those ideas and spend a bit of time fleshing them out – is this even worth a post? Is it perhaps more than one post? What research do I need to do to make it work?

That process might take twenty minutes, but I've usually discarded three or four ideas along the way and fleshed out three or four more to the point that I know what I'm going to write. From there, I never find myself "lost" at work – I know what tasks I need to do, I execute them, and I keep on rolling to the next one.

I might have spent the first twenty minutes of my day not moving forward at all on any projects, which seems bad. But the time invested in time management pays off – I don't have to worry about such details as the day goes on, allowing myself to focus on just getting things done. Thus, by the six hour mark, I'm usually far ahead in terms of my work if I've done that planning. The big part? I've drastically reduced my wasted time.

The end result? If I'm a couple hours ahead, I now have hours I can add to my personal life. Or, perhaps I can use them to work ahead, giving those personal hours more of a cushion in case something happens. Maybe I can spend an hour getting in touch with others, building relationships that will really pay off over time. Maybe I can work on another project that might lead to more earnings or more readers, both of which shore up the valuable parts of my life.

Time is money, and when you manage your time well, you manage your money well, too.

How do you do that?

VALUABLE TECHNIQUES FOR MANAGING TIME

1. Start your day off with some planning.

Make a list of what you need to get done today – usually four or so things. Don't just make a 1, 2, 3, 4 list, though – investigate each one for a few minutes and make sure you have the information, ideas, and materials you need to actually execute each item. That might mean spending five or ten minutes on the basic framework of a task, but doing that now means you won't burn an hour chasing snipe later on. Also, that list of things to do will keep you from burning time in the middle of the day wondering what's best to do next.

2. Alternate between multi-tasking and single-tasking sessions.

Multi-tasking works well for some tasks – phone calls, emails, filing, and so forth. Those are tasks that usually aren't mentally taxing at all, and thus can be done two or more at a time. However, the meat and potatoes of your work usually does require your focus – and doing that with interruptions makes it take longer and reduces the quality of your work. Take a few periods during your day, turn off your communication routes (turn off your phone, close your email program, etc.) for an hour or so and bear down on a task that needs to be done. When it's finished, go back into multitasking mode and get caught up on your messages and information.

3. Meditate.

This sounds counterintuitive, but it really works. It's easy, later in the day, to "zone out" – you're mentally (and perhaps physically) worn out. Many people keep pushing, but they find themselves losing three minutes here and three minutes there because they space off – and this will often spread into the evening's personal time. Instead, try meditating for fifteen or twenty minutes near the end of your work day. Just sit in a chair and relax, I almost always find myself refreshed and alert after doing this.

4. Write down the things on your mind.

Keep a notebook and pen near you at all times. Whenever something pops into your head that you need to do later or think about later, jot it down immediately. Then, a few times a day, leaf through the notebook and take care of the things jotted down there. Throw down anything and everything – a word you want to look up, a personal task you need to take care of, a person you want to get in touch with. Getting these things out of your head and onto paper means you can spend far less mental energy trying to remember it – and use that energy instead focusing on your current task and getting that done as well as you can.

Find ways to spend your free time that simultaneously help you grow as a person and bring you enjoyment.

Reading literature that really pushes your mind is one example. Going for a jog is another example. Almost any social activity falls into this group, too – learning how to interact with more people is invaluable. Such activities bleed back into the rest of your day – they increase your energy at work, improve your mental acuity, and raise the bar on your ability to interact with others and network. Putting forth a little effort to find enjoyable ways to spend your spare time that also help you to grow pays off over and over again.

Remember, time is money – so stop wasting it.

Rule #11

Take Care of Your Things

Whenever I'm in a financially destitute area, I start seeing many of the same things.

I see homes that are creaky, often with paint falling off. I see front yards and back yards full of items left out in the rain to fall apart. I see cars in poor shape, a mixture of rust and lots of hard miles on them. I see overgrown and patchy lawns. I see air conditioning units that sound like they're about ready to explode, covered in dust and cobwebs.

In short, I see a lot of items that people own that simply have no care given to them at all. Unsurprisingly, these items will have to be replaced sooner than they would with even a little bit of TLC (Tender Love and Care) – or else they are items that were bought completely frivolously, were barely used, and will never be replaced.

The true cost of poor maintenance

A poorly-maintained air conditioner sucks down more energy than one that's well maintained – adding to your energy bill – and it fails quicker – adding to your repair and replacement bills.

A house with paint falling off needs to be repainted and treated or else you open yourself up to additional weathering from the environment, reducing the lifespan and resale value of the house itself.

Items left out in the yard? The sun bleaches them, the rain wears away at them, and they live a very short life. You'll be buying a new basketball before you know it.

I'm not picking on people who make these lifestyle choices. Instead, **I'm drawing a connection between their financial state and the way they treat their stuff.** With every item that sits out there and dilapidates, some of their financial resources are simply blowing away. Taken together, those resources provide the opportunity to have the things you dream of.

Take the air conditioner, as just an obvious example. An average air conditioner has a lifespan of fifteen years. If you maintain it well, you can likely stretch that a few more years – let's say eighteen years. If you do nothing with it, the lifespan will be shorter – say, twelve years.

An average central air unit uses 161 kilowatt hours during an average summer month. A well maintained conditioner, with clear vents, might shave 5% off of that, while an unmaintained unit might add 5% more to that.

Replacing such a unit will cost about £4,000.

So, what's the total cost over a thirty year period? If you maintain your unit well, you will have replaced it once and be two-thirds of the way towards replacing a second unit – a total unit cost of £6,667. Over thirty summers, you will have used 13,765 kilowatt-hours of energy – at a price of ten cents per kilowatt hour, that's £1,376.50. Your total cost? £8,043.50.

What about a poorly-maintained unit? You will have replaced your unit twice and be halfway towards a third replacement – a unit cost of £10,000. Over thirty summers, you will have used 15,215 kilowatt-hours of energy – at a price of ten cents per kilowatt hour, that's £1,512.50. Your total cost £11,512.50.

Spending a few minutes each spring and a few minutes each fall making sure the air conditioning unit is clean and in proper working order saves a family £3,469 over a period of thirty years.

Start carrying that across other expenditures; your house - he wood, roof, and foundation; your equipment, your clothing and shoes, your vehicles etc. All of these things have significant savings that come around when you put even a small amount of care into maintenance. Over a decade, you can easily save tens of thousands of pounds by properly maintaining your belongings.

All earned by spending a minute or two here or there

taking care of your stuff.

Save money by taking care of your things

It's pretty easy to do, actually. Most of the home maintenance tasks you do are pretty simple ones – they're just somewhat numerous and are easy to forget at times.

What you'll find when you do this is that things run just a bit better. Your air conditioner doesn't kick on quite as often. Your dryer runs efficiently. Your appliances rarely seem to have problems. Your refrigerator doesn't run constantly.

All of those little things add up to a bit of energy savings now – and a lot of savings later, when you're not replacing these expensive items.

You can carry this through to more items in your home as well. Take your shoes, for example. Making sure they're clean, treating expensive shoes well, and storing them in places where they won't continually take bumps is a good step towards extending their life. Or your lawnmower – taking the time to occasionally sharpen the blades and check the oil reduces the wear and tear on the engine greatly, saving you money on gas and also on replacing your mower. Or your roof – keep those gutters clean and your roof will take less wear and tear. **It doesn't take much time to do these things, either.**

Compare the two minutes here or there spent doing maintenance to the time you'd have to invest buying a new unit early – research, shopping around, and so on – and the time begins to balance out, too.

You can easily expand this philosophy beyond the material. Take care of your relationships. Take care of your work contacts. Take care of your career. Take care of your body.

There are other positive effects, as well. Take the environment, for example. The fewer items you replace, the fewer things that wind up in landfills. The less energy you use, the fewer fossil fuels you burn.

There are also the positive psychological benefits of taking care of your things. In many ways, it's akin to taking care of yourself psychologically. You're doing positive things with your time which fills you with positive feelings all around. You're improving your things that you value, which by extension improves you.

Adding together all of these benefits, I find it to be essential to take the time to maintain the things you have.

Rule #12

Do It Yourself

Do you ever wonder whether to pay for services or whether to do things yourself?

One big caveat, right off the bat: I'm not claiming that you should do everything yourself. There are certainly situations where paying others to do things for you is beneficial, and those opportunities become more prevalent as your income rises.

However, the more things you do for yourself, the less money you spend on overpriced services.

This spreads across more avenues of life than you might initially think. "I don't pay for a lawn service," you might think, "and I'll never hire a maid or a cook." It goes far beyond that.

Alternatives to paying for common services

When you go out to eat, you pay for someone to serve you. Much of your cost of the meal isn't in the food – it's in the cost of the cook to prepare it and the waiter to bring it to your table. Instead, cook the same meal at home. Almost always, it will be significantly less expensive – and often healthier. Even more surprising, it often won't take you as long as your trip to the restaurant took.

When you buy produce at the grocery store, you pay for people to serve you. Most of your cost comes from people picking the vegetables and people transporting them to you. Instead, why not have a small vegetable garden in the back? It can be a bit of a time sink (but less than you might think if you don't garden), but the costs can be extremely low, particularly for the quantity of vegetables you can get from a good garden.

When you shell out for snow removal, you're backing away from a great opportunity for winter exercise – and losing some cash along the way as well.

When you go get an oil change, you're paying for someone to unscrew a couple caps and dump liquid out of a jug. Why not buy your own oil, get a pan, and do it yourself? It doesn't take long and you won't be given a sales pitch along the way.

When you call up the plumber or the electrician, you're likely paying someone to handle something that could be figured out from a YouTube video. If nothing else, it's worth a few minutes to check YouTube for a how-to video to see if your problem can be easily fixed.

In each case, the same theme is clear: **you pay a high price for someone else to do something for you.**

The cost of time

One common counterargument to this is the idea that a person's time is more valuable than that. "My time is worth more than the cost of just paying someone else to do it."

Here's the catch, though – what are you replacing that time with? Are you doing something really productive with it? Or are you recouping that time with an extra episode of a sitcom?

Often, the argument that one's time is more valuable is a front for laziness. It's simply easier to throw cash at a problem. While that may be true on one level, step back for a minute and look at it from a distance. Do the people who succeed in life succeed by taking the lazy route? Rarely.

That's not to say that there isn't value in relaxation time. Unquestionably, there is. However, there is an enormous gulf between relaxation and laziness. Relaxation refreshes you and makes you ready to succeed in other aspects of life. Laziness passes time and merely reinforces laziness. Sitting down to relax and enjoy a television program that really fulfils you is relaxation. Flipping on the cable box to see what's on? Not so much.

If you're truly replacing a drudgery task with something that fulfils you deeply or earns a much better income than the cost of the service, then by all means, consider it. Just keep the bigger picture in mind and make sure you're not paying a lot of money so that you can idle away the time.

Other benefits of doing things yourself

Doing things for yourself also has big psychological benefits. It shows you that you actually can do these things for yourself and improves your self-worth. It increases your skill set. It often gets you moving and applying your mind and your body together in a task. These are all enormous benefits that aren't derived from simply throwing cash at a problem.

In the end, the personal and financial benefits of doing things yourself add up to an enormous benefit for the time you invest in it. The next time you have something that you could do yourself that you're about to pay someone else to take care of, step back and ask yourself if this is really the best move for you.

Rule #13
Find And Work Toward Your True Passions

I've watched it over and over again, the people that succeed in a particular career path are the people who are able to tap into their natural passions and aim that fire hose into their professional life. They know what they love and they find ways to translate that into a way to make a living. Sometimes they make a nice income – and that's awesome. At other times, they earn just enough to get by – and that's awesome, too.

What matters is that, in both cases, it's a joy to get out of bed in the morning and get started on your day. Your work itself fills you with joy and excitement. When you reach that point, the line between work and play disappears – you're happy doing whatever your day throws at you. That has a value that can't be measured in pounds and pennies. It transforms your life.

I hear from many people who claim this is impossible. It's not. Every single day, I get out of bed, excited to speak. If anything, I speak more each day than I did when my passion for speaking was still new. I know others who feel the same way about what they do. It makes them want to get out of bed in the morning and get started. When you feel that passion surging through you, it makes a lot of the little difficulties of life not matter too much.

If this seems completely alien to you, you simply haven't discovered your passion yet.

Figure Out Your Passions

1. Maximize your health.

Eat well. Get some exercise. Get away from any and all situations that are emotionally holding you back. Get plenty of sleep. Without these pieces in place, it will be hard for you to open up to new opportunities and directions.

2. Ask many questions.

If you come across something of interest to you, ask. Follow up with more questions until you're satisfied – at least for the moment. Research interesting topics online, do things like a "Wikipedia stumble" – start at a general topic you're thinking about, and then click on whatever article in Wikipedia that's most interesting to you – and keep reading and following links.

3. Ignore what's "cool."

Remember the idea that you should stop trying to impress other people in rule #4? It comes through big time here. If you enjoy it, it doesn't matter what others think. Don't be afraid to dive into something that seems exciting to you over a fear that others might find it "dorky." Their label says more about them than it does about the activity.

4. Dabble in everything.

If something seems interesting, try it. You might not find it enjoyable or you might find it fascinating. It's often hard to tell the difference until you dive in. For example, having a garden might seem interesting, but until you try it, it's hard to tell whether it's just conceptually interesting to you (but not necessarily in practice) or something that you truly enjoy.

5. When something piques your interest, dig in.

You try it. You like it. So try it again, and again. There are many things that seem quite fun on the first shot, but grow boring quickly as you hit "the dip" (where the newness wears off but you're not very good at it). If you're passionate about something, you won't mind that dip.

6. Associate with others that share this growing passion of yours.

Look for events in your area where people might be involved with this interest. Look for groups online where people are talking about this activity. Join in, share your thoughts, and ask questions. Nothing's better for fostering a growing interest than a group of like-minded people.

7. If it dries up, don't push it.

True passions are sustaining – you'll keep coming back to

them because you want to. If you no longer want to engage in it, don't make yourself. Just back away and find another path. You may find yourself returning in the future, or you may find yourself on a completely different path.

You'll know your passion when you find it

It'll ring inside of you like a hammer hitting a church bell. It'll consume your thoughts and your activities, even if you're not very good at it yet. You'll get up each morning excited to do more. This is how I feel about writing, for one.

What do you do if you discover your passion, but there doesn't seem to be any way to translate that into income? After all, you have to pay the bills, and even though you've found something you love so much you'd be happy to do it every day, it doesn't put food on the table.

There are countless avenues for channelling that passion into income. However, almost all of these paths require you to start doing it on a part-time basis. Give up the frivolous things you were spending your evenings on and devote some of that time to a new path.

PROFIT FROM YOUR PASSION

Blog

Start a blog on the topic you're passionate about.

Share something new every day on there. Put a few adverts on the site to earn a bit of revenue.

Teach / tutor

If you have patience, hang out your shingle and volunteer to teach your passion to others. This is a great avenue for a passionate musician.

Provide services

Maybe you've found that you're passionate about a particular task that others find to be drudgery – scooping snow or repairing computers. Sell these services directly to others.

Create videos

If you want to teach how to do the things you love, consider making videos and sharing them online. Put them on YouTube and make a simple blog to share the videos. If you start gathering followers, sign up for their rewards program and you can translate this into solid income.

Sell at farmers' markets

If you make things, from soap to bread to wicker baskets, you can likely do well selling the items at farmers markets. It's a great way to make some sales and meet people interested in what you're doing.

Write freelance articles / books

If you simply enjoy writing, practice and attempt to sell some of your best work as a freelancer. Expect plenty of rejections, but also expect feedback and suggestions, especially as you improve.

Develop projects through work

Take what you're passionate about and see how it can connect to your workplace. If you're into catering, volunteer to spend some work time getting catering set up for a work event. If you're into art, look for ways to incorporate your art into work projects.

Take classes

Work towards a degree in the area of your passion. It's a great way to get yourself into the marketplace and to connect with lots of like-minded folks.

Volunteer / apprentice

Don't be afraid to spend your spare time volunteering to share your passion with others. Time and time again, people who share their talents freely and build their skills find themselves in other opportunities to earn an income from it.

Sell by consignment

If you have a product to sell, talk to local sellers and see if they sell by consignment. They provide the space and the sales work for a cut of the revenue, while you get to focus on what you love.

Finding your passion is a life-changing event. It pushes you in new directions that fulfil you in ways you'd never expect. If you've never found your passion, you're missing out on life by not seeking it out.

Rule #14
Build Real Friendships and Relationships

I believe the fundamental unit of value in the modern world is relationships, and income derived from those relationships.

Think about it for a moment. What happens if your relationship with your boss and your co-workers sours? You lose your job – your income goes down. What happens if you build stronger relationships with your boss and your co-workers? Your income goes up – you get raises and promotions and bigger projects.

You can easily carry this over into your personal life, too. Let's say you're about to move. If you have a lot of real friends, a few phone calls will get you all the help you need. If you don't have these relationships, you'll be shelling out cash for a moving service (a big cost), or doing it yourself (a huge time sink).

This phenomenon pops up in pretty much every aspect of our lives. Food? If you have lots of relationships, you get a lot of dinner invites. Household supplies? If you have a lot of friends, at least one will have a bulk-discount membership and will likely split some bulk purchases with you. A leaky roof? If you have a good friend that's a carpenter and several other friends willing to hammer nails, you can likely get that roof fixed on the cheap. Entertainment? Swap piles of DVDs with your friends.

The list goes on and on.

From this, it's easy to see that building up a lot of real relationships with people is valuable. What do I mean by a real relationship? I'm referring to one where something of positive value is exchanged on a regular basis – useful advice, a helping hand, loaning of items, an ear to truly listen, and so on. Any relationship worth its salt has a healthy dose of positive exchanges of value with a minimum of negative exchanges like insults, backstabbing, gossip, incorrect advice, being an obstacle.

I confess that for a long time, I didn't know how to do this well at all. It wasn't that I thought other people should give me value in exchange for nothing – I just simply didn't understand the value of such exchanges. I was naturally quiet and it felt to me as though the effort expended in making myself reach out was much more than any value there was in what I might have to offer. In other words, introversion and a lack of self-confidence left me in a state where I didn't build many relationships.

Tips to Building Real and Honest Relationships

1. Open up a little.

If you're an introvert and prefer to be quiet, the best thing you can do for your life is to work on overcoming that nature. Talk to people. If you find this hard, bone up on techniques for basic conversation. Work on tactics that make you appear more confident, even if you aren't.

2. Surround yourself with people.

Go to where people are and open up. Attend conferences and conventions and meetings. If you hear someone talk who seems interesting, follow up directly with that person. Volunteer to present – it'll give lots of others a chance to hear you.

3. Host parties.

Start having dinner parties and backyard barbecues on a regular basis. Don't just invite the same old people, either – rotate the people you invite. Try to mix it up, too – don't just invite the same circles. Mix the circles. This gives you the powerful opportunity to introduce people who may not know each other but may actually have a lot in common. If you don't know where to start, start with your neighbours and your current friends.

4. Keep in touch.

Make a regular habit of keeping in direct contact with people. My technique is simple: I keep a big list of people I want to maintain relationships with and I strive to contact people on that list on a regular basis. I let them know what I'm up to directly and ask what they're doing.

5. Give of yourself freely.

If someone needs help, help. Don't worry about "payback." Don't worry about what you might get out of it. Just help them. If you contact someone and find out they're stuck on a project, need a job, or need a helping hand in some other way, either provide that help yourself (if you can) or find someone who can provide that help and make the connection.

6. Ask for advice – and share what you get.

One thing I've found very useful is to treat my circle of friends like something of a help group. When I'm stuck on a big purchase or something like that, I ask a large group of friends for help and suggestions. I then compile all of that, figure out what's best for me, then take the best of the information and send it back to all of my friends, letting them know what I found out. This is almost universally valuable – people love participating to help a friend, they love getting that info back, and when I mention them, they sometimes make new connections themselves.

7. Show appreciation for help that you get.

At some point, you'll need some direct help from the people you've built relationships with (you'd be surprised how often they provide indirect help). When you do ask for that help, be thankful. Thank them for showing up, thank them for whatever help they provide, and do what you can to make their contribution easier – plenty of beverages, food, or anything else you can provide.

Doing these things over and over again will cause you to build a lot of stable, value-based relationships over time. Time and time again, those relationships will come through for you when you need them in your career and in your personal life.

Rule #15

Improve Yourself Every Chance You Get

Throughout my life, I've found that there are two kinds of people. One group seems to be constantly bored, idling away their days and waiting for life to come to them. The other group does the opposite – they're constantly busy, feel like there aren't enough hours in the day, and are out there chasing life.

I'm in that opposite group. I feel annoyed with myself when I see myself wasting time. I don't avoid relaxing and enjoying life by any means, but if I'm mentally and physically rested, I'd rather be doing something than just twiddling my thumbs. I'd rather be writing or researching something or reading for enrichment or doing something engaging with my wife or doing household chores or doing something engaging with my child.

Furthermore, when those avenues are full, I look for other ways to improve myself.

Why? Why not just kick back when things are finished up?

It's simple. The time I spend improving myself now always pays bigger dividends later. Self-improvement is an investment of time and energy instead of an investment of money, but both pay excellent returns. It can improve your health, your emotions, your career, and your financial state.

Ways to Improve Yourself and Your Quality of Life

Improve your health

Just walking thirty minutes a day for twelve years adds, on average, 1.3 healthy years to your life. That's 49 days of walking in exchange for 1.3 years of additional life – a brilliant trade. Doing more vigorous exercise can add even more – 3.7 years of life on average.

If you want to break it down, on average, a thirty minute walk will add almost five hours to your life. Go on a thirty minute walk each night after work and a single week's worth, on average, will add a day to your life. That's a profound argument for improving your health, even by taking simple steps.

This doesn't mean that you have to abandon more leisurely pursuits. One of my closest friends does sit-ups while watching television. Another friend has a treadmill that he walks on while reading magazines. They're not abandoning the things they like to do to mentally unwind, but they realize that mental unwinding doesn't mean you have to physically unwind, either. I like to jog while listening to podcasts or audio books. While running, my mind is engaged – but that doesn't mean that I can't improve my body as well.

Improve your knowledge

Ideas are incredibly valuable and grow more valuable every day as society moves in a direction where creativity is rewarded. Knowledge is the base upon which creativity is built. Exposure to new ideas and new angles in a mix with the unique set of ideas and life experiences you already have make it more and more likely that you'll be able to produce unique ideas – and those unique ideas can be incredibly valuable.

One powerful way to do this is to read, which I suppose, is what you're doing right now. Take on a book that challenges you and pushes the way you think. I like to read books that advocate positions I don't agree. These books force me to understand other perspectives and, at the same time, re-evaluate and strengthen and perhaps change my own.

Another effective way to get there is through conversation with a person willing to engage ideas. Share your thoughts, listen to what they share, and debate their relative merits. Accept that criticism of an idea that you presented is not criticism of you, but of the idea itself.

Improve your transferable skills

Transferable skills are the types of skills that fit well in almost any career path. They are always worthwhile to build - communication skills, time management skills, creativity and leadership.

How can you do these things? Well, you might try implementing a new time management system in your life. Invest some time in figuring out getting things done. Or you might volunteer to take a leadership position in a community group. Play a brainstorming game with friends, like or a strategic game - they will help you with communication skills, creativity, and logical thought.

Look at the things you choose to do in your "down time" and ask yourself if they're also helping you build transferable skills in a subtle way. Then, choose activities that you really enjoy that do build these skills. You'll grow a lot more playing brainstorming games with creative people than you will watching a sitcom by yourself.

Improve your personal nature

Knowing who you are – your strengths, your weaknesses, your joys, your sorrows, makes it a lot easier to navigate the minefield of life. It's well worth your time to figure out who you are and what you truly value.

Spend some time being introspective. Ask yourself how you honestly feel about the elements in your life. Are these things bringing you joy or sadness? Why? What elements, you ask? Look at everything: your health, your relationships, your activities, your possessions, and so on.

This type of introspection can be very difficult. Often, we want to feel certain ways about certain things and, on some level, we convince ourselves that we do. Digging through that, figuring out our true feelings, and acting on them result in nothing but life improvement.

Improve your relationships

Most relationships need some amount of care and feeding, but in the busy nature of modern life, it's easy to overlook the care and feeding that some of our most important relationships require.

Take some time and just talk to your spouse about how life is going. Give your mother a long phone call. Get in touch with your siblings. Look up some of your close friends that you've drifted away from over time. Listen to what they're saying – don't just look at it as an excuse to list what you're up to. Those relationships are invaluable, and any time spent maintaining them will pay off in surprising ways over time.

Here's the real message: the difference between the successful and the non-successful appears in how they "waste" their time. People who succeed spend almost all of their time doing something that in some way improves themselves, their relationships, or their career situation. That's not accomplished by idling.

Rule #16

Make Giving a Lifestyle

Charity – in fact, giving of any kind – is often hard to explain in a general sense. Many people fail to see the purpose of giving. "What does it do for me?" they'll ask, and it's difficult to point to how charity brings you a discrete, specific, calculable return.

Instead, giving is a reflection of what truly matters to you in the world. It's your opportunity to actually make a tangible difference in an area that matters to you. Seeing that your effort has created change in someone's life – or created slight change in a lot of lives – is incredibly powerful.

The Power of Giving

Figure out what is important to you

This comes back to your central values. Perhaps you're impassioned about the environment and wish to take action to reduce carbon emissions. Perhaps you want to protect animal habitats. Perhaps you're fuelled by a desire to help people in famine situations – or in natural disasters. Perhaps you're committed to childhood education. Or maybe you just want to help out disadvantaged people in your own community. There are countless other causes that different people find valuable – yours may or may not be on this list.

Sometimes it can feel overwhelming – there are

so many things out there that deserve a gift that it's easier to fall into "analysis paralysis." You can't decide, so you choose to do nothing at all.

Just because a reason to give is worthwhile doesn't mean that it's the one you have to give to. Spend some time figuring out what matters the most to you. Is it the environment? Is it education? Is it famine and world food distribution? Is it poverty in your community? It could be any of these – or something else.

Once you've figured out what matters most to you, look only at ways to give in that area. For example, if I'm concerned about poverty in my community, I might dig into Habitat for Humanity and the local food bank. If I'm concerned about education, I can get involved with the local school district.

A small amount counts

People often argue that the small amount that they can contribute won't make a difference. If you're in that situation, look for ways where you can see that your small gift can make a change.

Give £10 worth of food to the local food bank, and then volunteer there. See for yourself that the food you purchased is going to a family that really needs it. Your gift directly put food on the table for those children.

Take £30 and use it to plant a tree in a park somewhere (obviously, after getting permission). Water it yourself and watch it grow. That tree will help clean the air and will provide shade and natural beauty for the people in the park, and you can see with your own eyes how it benefits others.

Keep a £20 bill in your pocket and wait until you see someone who's really in a pinch, then just put that £20 in their hand. Watch what happens next – their emotional reaction, the story they tell you. You made a difference.

Giving doesn't always mean money

Give your time, too. Spend an afternoon building a Habitat for Humanity house in your community. Spend two hours volunteering at the food bank in your community. Spend an afternoon at a homeless shelter.

The secret behind giving

As you give to something that truly matters to you, you feel incredibly good. That good feeling radiates throughout your life. People pick up on your good feelings and they respond better to you.

Your gift also contributes to the happiness of others. Children and families enjoy that tree you planted. A family makes a dinner out of your donation to that food bank. A family is able to finally have a home of their own thanks to your labour on the Habitat for Humanity project.

Someone's life becomes better. Their outlook moves just a bit higher. They make a few better choices in their life: the family decides that a family afternoon in the park is pretty nice because of the cool shade and decide to do it again. These family bonds a bit more and, later on, their child will make a difficult, positive choice because of that closer bond.

Life is full of these little chaotic effects. Our actions cause many, many things to happen, many of which we don't see. Giving of ourselves freely in a positive way sends out ripples of good events, and over time, those ripples come back to you and to everyone you care about. You might not see the direct effect, but those indirect effects echo throughout your life.

Give what you can, without regrets. The positive benefits echo throughout your life, the lives of everyone you care about, and lives you've never crossed. Walk away knowing that the work of your life has gone to truly make, the world a better place.

Don't forget the tax benefit too!

Donations to charity from individuals are tax free. You can get tax relief if you donate:

- Through Gift Aid
- Straight from your wages or pension, through
- Payroll Giving

Rule #17

Have A Savings Plan

Financial priorities change over time, but a good savings plan lasts a lifetime. These five tips will keep you on track.

It's no secret that your financial priorities change over the course of your life. In your teens you might save for a car, in your 30s you might save for your kids' education, and by your 40s and 50s you're more focused on your retirement. However, to achieve any of these goals, you need a solid savings plan, one that keeps you on track for your long-term goals, and one that will see you through any economic downturns that may happen along the way.

Consolidating your accounts is a simple solution, which makes it a good place to start. It'll save you money on fees and reduce the risk of losing track of accounts and incurring charges. Those savings might seem small, but they add up fast.

Of course the key to any savings plan is to start early. That way you can take full advantage of the power of compound interest. "A little bit saved each month starting at age 25 beats a lot saved every year starting at age 50," says Heather Franklin, a certified financial planner in Toronto. "Every day you wait to put a savings plan in place could affect the lifestyle you want."

FOLLOWING THESE FIVE ESSENTIAL STEPS WILL HELP YOU CREATE A SUCCESSFUL SAVINGS PLAN:

1. Identify what you are saving for

You can't get to your destination unless you have a road map. Having a clear objective of what you are saving for is the first step, whether it's for a family vacation, a TV or second family car. "People know they have to save, but if they can visualize their financial goals, it really helps," says Sheila Munch, a CFP and owner of Durham Financial in Oshawa, Ont. It also helps to write down each objective with the amount you want to save and a target date for reaching your goal. "Don't rush this part," she says. "This helps ensure you'll succeed."

2. Determine how much you can save

Whether you make £50,000 or £150,000 a year, you need a snapshot of how much you're spending. That's where a budget comes in. Once in place, you can determine how much you can allocate to savings or if you need to rein in your spending. "If 5% of income is all you can afford, start there," says Franklin. "Then increase it to 10% or 15%." If you're unsure how much you should be saving talk with an adviser who can help you build a budget and show you ways to save that you may not have considered, like consolidating or restructuring debt to lower your interest costs.

3. Choose the appropriate solutions

There are many ways to save and invest your money, including savings accounts, Guaranteed Investment Certificates (GICs), mutual funds, exchange-traded funds (ETFs)-the list goes on. The trick is picking the one that works for you. Choosing the right savings vehicle will depend on how much you can save, how frequently you plan to add to your savings, and how quickly you may need to access that money.

For short-term goals, focus on safety and liquidity rather than growth. Savings accounts (including ISA Accounts), high-interest savings accounts are good options. Picking the right investments for medium-term goals can be more challenging, because you need to strike a balance between protecting your assets and growing them to offset inflation. As a general rule, the more time you have to reach a financial goal, the more investment risk you can afford. More risk means more volatility, but if you have 15 years or more to meet your goals, you should be able to ride out any market downturns.

4. Make it automatic

If you don't see the money, you're less likely to spend it. Once you know how much you want to tuck away-say 5% or 10% of your after-tax salary-set up an automatic transfer to a separate savings account or investment account as soon as you're paid. Even small amounts count. For instance, £200 a month earning 2% annually will grow to £2,426 after the first year, to £7,424 after the third year, and to £12,625 in just five years. "It will hurt for the first three months, but after that you'll get used to it, it's absolutely pain-free saving."

5. Monitor your progress

Take a few minutes every few months to see if you're meeting your savings goals. "If you get a salary increase, add it to your savings," "It shouldn't be an opportunity to spend more." There's more to saving than cutting your spending and setting aside that money. A host of government programs, for instance, have been set up to help you through almost every stage of your life-you just have to know how to take advantage of them.

Rule #18

Track Your Progress

One of the first things I did when I started turning my financial situation around is to start keeping track of my net worth over time. Each week (and later each month), I calculated the value of all of my assets, all of my debts, and the difference between the two (my net worth).

Later, when I began to try to improve my physical shape, I started keeping careful track of several metrics: my weight, my resting heartbeat, and the number of miles I was walking and jogging.

I like to call it the "keeping score" effect. Almost always, it becomes more fun to work towards a difficult goal if you have some sort of method of comparing your progress to the progress of others, or comparing your current state with your state in the past. You can see the improvement clearly – when you look and see that your net worth is up £10,000 compared to last year or you see your average mile is more than a minute faster than it was a couple months ago, it feels enormous. It's a giant rush.

The entire point here is to keep yourself motivated towards your goals. Keeping score keeps your big goals front and centre in your mind. Combining that with a visual reminder of your goal can be particularly powerful, as it keeps your goal front and centre in your mind and also demonstrate your progress clearly.

There are countless tools out there to help you keep track of your personal finance progress.

4 Worthwhile Areas to Track Your Progress In

Track your assets

For me, I only include the assessed value of my home plus the balances of any investment accounts and savings accounts I have. In a normal month, I expect this amount to move up slowly over the previous month, meaning I'm actually saving money. Some months see a precipitous drop, though – for example, if I buy a car, that's usually a pretty big money hit, since I don't include my car as part of my assets since they depreciate so much.

Track your debts

This is important, if you're trying to plow your way through a debt repayment plan. Each month, you record the balance of each debt, and then add them up. If you're actually pushing well on that debt repayment plan, the total balance of your debts should significantly drop each month. If you don't see your debt dropping, you need to take a serious look at what's going on.

Track your net worth

This one's simple – just add up your assets and subtract all of your debts from the total. Obviously, each month, you want your net worth to be higher than the previous month. I like to make a note of the difference from month to month and I strive to increase this difference each month.

Track your spending

Whenever you spend, jot it down. Keep track of all of it and, at the end of the month, add it up. Even more important, divide that spending into categories – utilities, necessary food, eating out, entertainment, books – and total up each category. This technique is powerful because it shows you the areas where your spending is out of control and you need to tighten up.

As I mentioned earlier, when you keep track of your progress in this way, it becomes a huge aid for setting goals.

SET SHORT TERM GOALS

Here are three ways I have used the above data to set short term goals for myself, pushing me to new heights:

1. I want my net worth growth to be better this month than last.

Let's say my net worth goes up £1,000 from June to July. I then want my net worth growth from July to August to be £1,001 or more. Obviously, I can't control the growth of the stock market, but I can control my spending impulses.

2. I want to cut my spending in this specific category by 50% next month.

If I notice that I spent more than I thought in a certain area last month – like books, for example, or on eating out – I set a goal for the next month to reduce my spending in that category by a decisive amount without jacking up my spending elsewhere.

3. I want my debt to drop more this month than last month.

Doing this works hand in hand with my net worth goal, but in a slightly more specific way. I'll push hard to find a few extra pounds that month to roll into a debt payment.

I've also found that the social aspect of such tracking and goal setting is powerful. If you like to do this online, Wesabe is an incredibly interesting and powerful tool for sharing your information and comparing it to the progress of others. You can offer encouragement to others, let them encourage you, and push towards goals together.

I'm highly partial to doing this offline, though. Find a personal finance buddy and meet together regularly to encourage each other, share your progress and your challenges, and offer useful tips to each other. For me, the reality of meeting someone face to face makes such progress tracking more real – and it also adds a stronger edge of competitiveness to the mix.

In the end, keeping track of your personal finance progress is crucial. It shows you quite clearly where you've been, how far you've come, and where you need to go. It helps you see the areas where you're successful – and points out the areas where you need more work. It constantly pushes you forward to bigger and better things. In the end, watching your steps helps you follow that trail straight to your dreams, whether it's a financial dream or a dream in any aspect of your life.

GLOSSARY

'Asset'
A resource with economic value that an individual, corporation or country owns or controls with the expectation that it will provide future benefit.

Capital'
Financial assets or the financial value of assets, such as cash.

"Capital" can mean many things. Its specific definition depends on the context in which it is used. In general, it refers to financial resources available for use. Companies and societies with more capital are better off than those with less capital.

'Consignment'
An arrangement whereby goods are left in the possession of another party to sell. Typically, the consignor receives a percentage of the sale (sometimes a very large percentage). Consignment deals are made on a variety of products - from artwork, to clothing, to books. In recent years, consignment shops have become rather trendy, especially those offering specialty products, infant wear and high-end fashion items.

'Debt'
An amount of money borrowed by one party from

another. Many corporations/individuals use debt as a method for making large purchases that they could not afford under normal circumstances. A debt arrangement gives the borrowing party permission to borrow money under the condition that it is to be paid back at a later date, usually with interest.

'Inflation'
Inflation is the rate at which the general level of prices for goods and services is rising and, consequently, the purchasing power of currency is falling. Central banks attempt to limit inflation, and avoid deflation, in order to keep the economy running smoothly.

'Net Worth'
The amount by which assets exceed liabilities. Net worth is a concept applicable to individuals and businesses as a key measure of how much an entity is worth. A consistent increase in net worth indicates good financial health; conversely, net worth may be depleted by annual operating losses or a substantial decrease in asset values relative to liabilities. In the business context, net worth is also known as book value or shareholders' equity.

'Profit'
A financial benefit that is realized when the amount of revenue gained from a business activity exceeds the expenses, costs and taxes needed to sustain the activity. Any profit that is gained goes to the business's owners, who may or may not decide to spend it on the business.

'Savings'
According to Keynesian economics, the amount left over when the cost of a person's consumer expenditure is subtracted from the amount of disposable income that he or she earns in a given period of time.

About the Author

Felix Makanjuola Jr is an Entrepreneur, Inspirational Speaker, Best Selling Author and Life Coach. His immense wealth of knowledge gained as an Entrepreneur and Trainer brings an added dimension of originality, relevance and insightfulness to his teachings.

Felix trained as a lawyer and was called to the English Bar in 2007. His flair for business started at an early age as a result of social circumstances around him. These made him seek out ways to manage his limited resources and maximise it.

He is appointed on various boards as chairman, trustee and CEO of non-governmental organisations and companies.

He has a passion for developing and empowering people to be the very best they can be and his trademark dynamism injects 'life' and restoration everywhere he goes.

Felix, his wife Victoria and their son Elnathan live in Swansea United Kingdom.

For resources and more information visit:
www.felixmakjr.com

www.felixmakjr.com

www.ingramcontent.com/pod-product-compliance
Lightning Source LLC
Chambersburg PA
CBHW071005160426
43193CB00012B/1930